Jobs if You Like...

Building Things

Charlotte Guillain

Heinemann
LIBRARY
Chicago, Illinois

H www.capstonepub.com
Visit our website to find out more information about Heinemann-Raintree books.

To order:
☎ Phone 800-747-4992
💻 Visit www.capstonepub.com
to browse our catalog and order online.

Edited by Rebecca Rissman, Daniel Nunn, and Adrian Vigliano
Designed by Steve Mead
Picture research by Mica Brancic
Originated by Capstone Global Library
Printed and bound in China by South China Printing Company

16 15 14 13 12
10 9 8 7 6 5 4 3 2 1

Library of Congress Cataloging-in-Publication Data
Guillain, Charlotte.
  Building things / Charlotte Guillain.—1st ed.
    p. cm.—(Jobs if you like...)
  Includes bibliographical references and index.
  ISBN 978-1-4329-6805-2 (hardback)—ISBN 978-1-4329-6816-8 (pbk.) 1. Industrial arts—Vocational guidance—Juvenile literature. 2. Engineering—Vocational guidance—Juvenile literature. 3. Building—Vocational guidance—Juvenile literature. I. Title.
  TS149.G85 2012
  670.23—dc23   2011031925

Acknowledgments
We would like to thank the following for permission to reproduce photographs: Alamy pp. 15 (© Christian Lagerek), 25 (© EuroStyle Graphics), 10 (© Hemis), 21 (© Lubos Chlubny); Getty Images pp. 24 (Bill Pugliano), 23 (Marco Secchi), 26 (Cultura/Zero Creatives); Glow Images pp. 4 (Blend/Eric Raptosh Photography), 18 (Corbis/© Ariel Skelley), 17 (Corbis/© LWA-Sharie Kennedy), 27 (Corbis/© Roger Ressmeyer), 7 (Corbis/© Somos Images), 19 (Cultura/© Monty Rakusen), 13 (Imagebroker RM), 22 (Imagebroker RM), 6 (PhotoAlto Premium/Laurence Mouton); London 2012 p. 5; Shutterstock pp. 16 (© Dmitriy Shironosov), 12 (© Kacso Sandor), 20 (© Marten Czamanske), 9 (© Ollirg), 14 (© Olly), 8 (© Stanislav Komogorov), 11 (© Filip Fuxa).

Cover photo of a builder in hardhat sawing reproduced with permission of Getty Images (UpperCut Images/Bounce).

Every effort has been made to contact copyright holders of material reproduced in this book. Any omissions will be rectified in subsequent printings if notice is given to the publisher.

Contents

Some words are shown in bold, **like this**. You can find out what they mean by looking in the glossary.

Why Does Building Things Matter?

Do you enjoy making models or building things? People are building things around us all the time. We need people to build our homes, schools, vehicles, parks, and many other things.

Many great toys can be used to build things.

Many people work hard to build things that look fantastic!

We need to know that the things people build are strong and safe. There are many different jobs that involve building in all sorts of ways. Read on to find out more!

Be an Architect

If you were an **architect**, you would plan and **design** buildings. You might have ideas for new homes, schools, offices, or airports. You might also help to repair old buildings.

Architects make detailed plans before building starts.

Architects think about who is going to use a building and what they need. They try to make their buildings strong, safe, and beautiful. Many architects try to design buildings that save energy and look good in their surroundings.

Architects make sure buildings are built following their plans.

Be a Civil Engineer

If you were a civil **engineer**, you could work on new bridges, roads, tunnels, airports, and other structures. You would work with **architects**, builders, and **surveyors** on each project.

Civil engineers help plan new projects and think about how much they will cost.

Civil engineers need to make sure their plans are clear. They need to be good at organizing lots of different people. They have to make sure projects run on time and don't cost too much money.

Structures like bridges can make people's lives safer and easier.

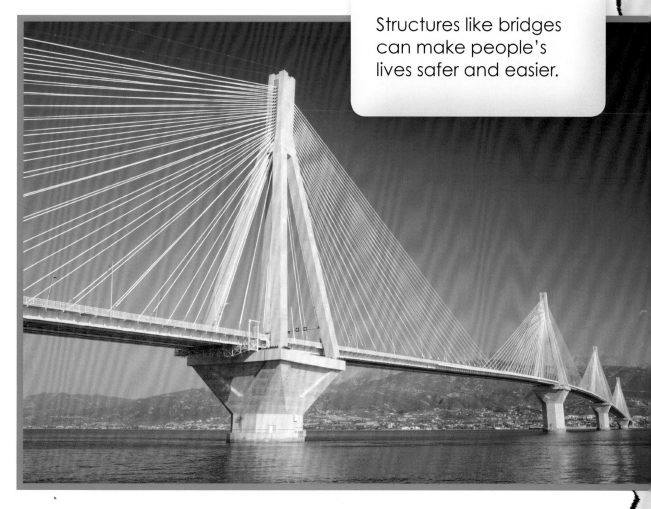

Be a Landscape Architect

If you were a **landscape architect**, your job would be to make open spaces look good. You might **design** the landscapes in parks, shopping centers, streets, or beside roads. You would visit the site and talk to people about what the area could look like.

Landscape architects think about many small details in their work.

Landscape architects think carefully about what plants to include in a space.

Landscape architects want people to enjoy open spaces and care for the environment. They choose the best trees and plants for a site and think about what people need. They make sure disabled people can move around the site.

11

Be an Electrician

Do you use a lot of electrical machines? If you do, then you need an electrician to make sure everything works properly and is safe. Electricians put electrical **wiring** and **circuits** into buildings so that we have all the electricity we need.

Electricians have special training to make sure they work safely.

Electricians have to check old wiring to make sure it is safe. They can also put fire alarms and other **equipment** into buildings. Some electricians make sure traffic lights work properly.

Electricians work with many interesting machines in their jobs.

Be a Mechanic

Are you interested in how machines work? If so, you could be a mechanic. Mechanics check and fix vehicles and machinery, such as cars, cranes, bulldozers, and tractors.

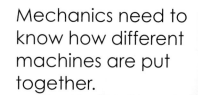

Mechanics need to know how different machines are put together.

Mechanics check engines, tires, and all the systems in a vehicle. Sometimes they have to take machines apart and repair them. Then they put the machines together again and test them to check that they work properly.

Mechanics need to use a lot of tools and **equipment**.

Be a Construction Manager

If you were a construction manager, you would be in charge of building work. You would work with a team of builders, making sure that the building follows the **architect's** plans. You would also make sure that the builders work safely.

Construction managers make sure that everyone is doing their job properly.

Construction managers need to be good at organizing their team.

Construction managers have to check that building work is done on time. They make sure that all the builders have the materials and **equipment** they need. They need to be good at talking to people and solving problems.

Be an Aerospace Engineer

If you love aircraft, then maybe you could be an aerospace **engineer**. You might work on airplanes, helicopters, or even space vehicles! You could come up with new ideas for ways to build better aircraft.

Aerospace engineers need to know how different parts of an aircraft work.

Aerospace engineers check and test an aircraft as it is built.

Aerospace engineers spend a lot of time **researching** and testing new ideas. They want new aircraft to travel fast and save energy. They use computers to **design** the plans for new aircraft. Then they check and test the vehicle as it is built.

19

Be a Welder

If you were a welder, you would build things out of metal. You might help to make buildings or vehicles. Another part of your job could be repairing machinery made of metal.

Welders have to wear special safety gear.

Welders take pieces of metal and join them together. They have to carefully check that the pieces are joined together properly. Sometimes they cut and join plastics and other materials.

Welders have to train to do special work.

Be a Set Designer

If you were a set designer, your job would be to **design** the **sets** on stage in the theater. You might also choose the backgrounds in films and television programs. You would start by reading the **script** to get ideas on how the set should look.

Some theater sets are moved around from place to place.

Set designers are always ready to work with new people to help tell different stories.

Set designers talk to the people designing costumes, lighting, and makeup. If the play or film is set in a different time or place, they find out about it. They sketch their ideas and then use a computer to design the sets.

Be a Motorsports Engineer

Do you love watching motor racing? Maybe you could be a motorsports **engineer**! You would **design** and develop new racing cars or motorcycles. You would spend a lot of time testing new ideas.

Motorsports engineers are always working with newer, faster technology.

Motorsports engineers are always looking for new ways to make cars go faster.

Motorsports engineers use computers to help them design new cars. They use new materials to make their cars go faster. They keep testing the cars when they have been built in order to make them as fast as possible.

Choosing the Right Job for You

When you decide what you want to do when you grow up, don't just think about school subjects. Think about what you enjoy doing. If you are interested in plants and the environment, you might like to be a **landscape architect**.

If you are crazy about vehicles, you might want to be an aerospace or motorsports **engineer**. There are so many different things to build, which means there is a job for everyone!

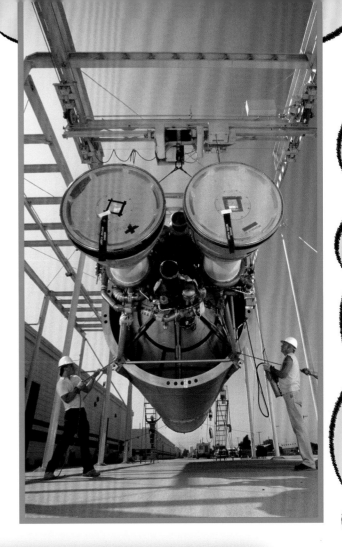

Five things you couldn't do without building things
- Live in your home
- Stand at the top of a skyscraper
- Switch on the lights or the television
- Ride a bicycle on a road
- Cross rivers on bridges

Building Things Job Chart

If you want to find out more about any of the jobs in this book, start here:

	Aerospace engineer	Architect	Civil engineer	Construction manager	
You need to:	Be good at solving problems	Be good at math and **designing**	Be good at organizing people	Be good at talking to people	
Best thing about it:	Seeing your designs in the air!	Seeing people use your buildings!	Building things that help people!	Seeing the finished building!	

Electrician	Landscape architect	Mechanic	Motorsport engineer	Set designer	Welder
Be good at following instructions	Know about plants and the environment	Know a lot about cars and machinery	Love cars	Be good at drawing	Be good at concentrating
Turning on the lights!	Making places look better!	Fixing problems!	When your car wins!	Seeing your work on the stage or screen!	You make things every day!

Glossary

architect person who designs buildings and directs how they are built

circuit path an electric current follows

design make or draw plans for something

engineer person who uses science and math to make tools, buildings, and machines

equipment something made to be used in a special way

landscape what is around us, for example hills, woods, or skyscrapers

research find as much information about something as possible

script words that are spoken in a play, film, or television program

set background in a play, film, or television program

surveyor person who studies the land or a building before construction work

wiring system of electric wires

Find Out More

Architecture for Children

www.archkidecture.org

This Website will teach you more about architecture and building design. You can read about words and materials used in architecture and get some ideas for building projects.

Welcome to ASCEville

www.asceville.org

Learn more about what a civil engineer needs to know at this Website.

KidsGardening

www.kidsgardening.org

You need to know a lot about plants if you want to be a landscape architect. This Website will help you learn about plants and gardening.

ZOOM Build

pbskids.org/zoom/activities/build

Visit this PBS Kids Website to find great ideas for things you can build. You can also send them your own great ideas!

Index